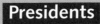

Presidents

# John Quincy Adams

## A MyReportLinks.com Book

Stephen Feinstein

MyReportLinks.com Books

an imprint of

Enslow Publishers, Inc. E

Box 398, 40 Industrial Road
Berkeley Heights, NJ 07922
USA

MyReportLinks.com Books, an imprint of Enslow Publishers, Inc.

**Library of Congress Cataloging-in-Publication Data**

Feinstein, Stephen.
   John Quincy Adams : A MyReportLinks.com Book / Stephen Feinstein.
     p. cm. — (Presidents)
   Includes bibliographical references and index.
   Summary: Discusses the personal life and political career of the son of the second
president of the United States, who became the sixth president. Includes Internet
links to Web sites, source documents, and photographs related to John Quincy
Adams.
   ISBN 0-7660-5002-5
   1. Adams, John Quincy, 176–-1848—Juvenile literature. 2. Presidents—United
States—Biography—Juvenile literature. [1. Adams, John Quincy, 1767–1848. 2.
Presidents.] I. Title. II. Series.

   E377 .F45 2002
   973.5'5'092—dc2 1
   [B]

                        2001004394

Printed in the United States of America

10 9 8 7 6 5 4 3 2 1

**To Our Readers:** We have done our best to make sure all Internet addresses in this book
were active and appropriate when we went to press. However, the author and the Publisher
have no control over, and assume no liability for, the material available on those Internet
sites or on other Web sites they may link to. The Publisher will try to keep the Report Links
that back up this book up to date on our Web site for three years from the book's
first publication date. Any comments or suggestions can be sent by e-mail to
comments@myreportlinks.com or to the address on the back cover.

**Photo Credits:** © Corel Corporation, pp. 1 (background), 3, 26; Courtesy of
MyReportLinks.com Books, p. 4; Courtesy of North Park University, p. 33;
Courtesy of The American President, pp. 38, 40; Courtesy of the Library of
Congress, p. 37; Courtesy of the Massachusetts Historical Society, pp. 16, 19, 24,
27; Courtesy of the National Archives and Records Administration, p. 13;
Courtesy of the National Museum of American History, Smithsonian Institution,
p. 44; Courtesy of the National Portrait Gallery, Smithsonian Institution, p. 43;
Courtesy of the Office of the Clerk, U.S. House of Representatives, p. 35;
Courtesy of the U.S. Dept. of State, pp. 28, 29; New Haven Colony Historical
Society, p. 12; U.S. Dept. of the Interior, National Park Service, Adams National
Historical Park, pp. 22, 39.

**Cover Photo:** © Corel Corporation; White House Collection, Courtesy of the
White House Historical Association.

# Contents

## MyReportLinks.com Books
### Great Books, Great Links, Great for Research!

MyReportLinks.com Books present the information you need to learn about your report subject. In addition, they show you where to go on the Internet for more information. The pre-evaluated Report Links, listed on **www.myreportlinks.com**, save hours of research time and link to dozens—even hundreds—of Web sites, source documents, and photos related to your report topic.

**To Our Readers:**

Each Report Link has been reviewed by our editors, who will work hard to keep only active and appropriate Internet addresses in our books and up to date on our Web site. However, the author and the Publisher have no control over, and assume no liability for, the material available on those Internet sites, or on other Web sites they may link to.

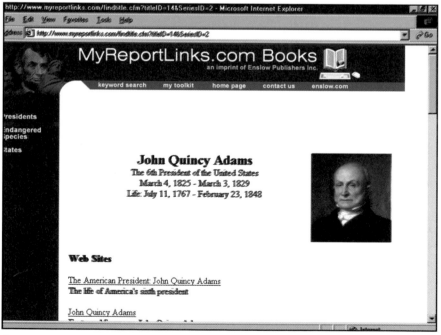

**Access:**

The Publisher will try to keep the Report Links that back up this book up to date on our Web site for three years from the book's first publication date. Please enter **PQA1227** if asked for a password.

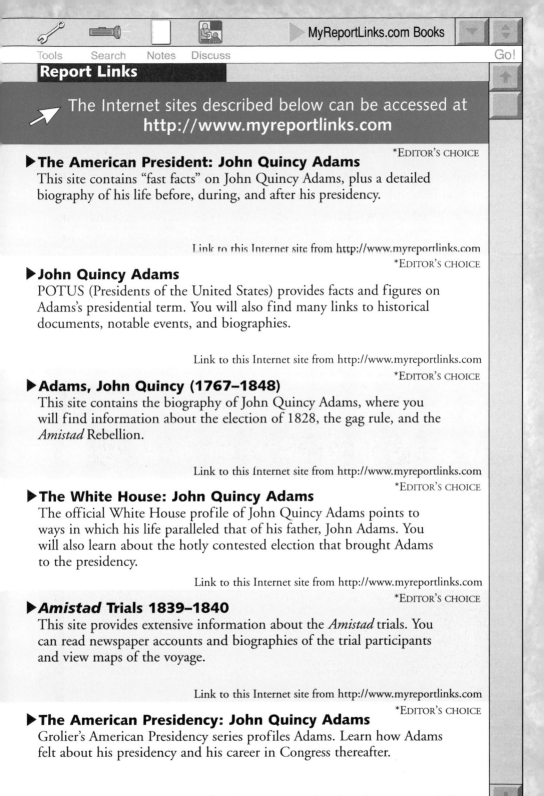

## Report Links

The Internet sites described below can be accessed at
**http://www.myreportlinks.com**

▶ **The American President: John Quincy Adams**    *EDITOR'S CHOICE
This site contains "fast facts" on John Quincy Adams, plus a detailed biography of his life before, during, and after his presidency.

Link to this Internet site from http://www.myreportlinks.com

▶ **John Quincy Adams**    *EDITOR'S CHOICE
POTUS (Presidents of the United States) provides facts and figures on Adams's presidential term. You will also find many links to historical documents, notable events, and biographies.

Link to this Internet site from http://www.myreportlinks.com

▶ **Adams, John Quincy (1767–1848)**    *EDITOR'S CHOICE
This site contains the biography of John Quincy Adams, where you will find information about the election of 1828, the gag rule, and the *Amistad* Rebellion.

Link to this Internet site from http://www.myreportlinks.com

▶ **The White House: John Quincy Adams**    *EDITOR'S CHOICE
The official White House profile of John Quincy Adams points to ways in which his life paralleled that of his father, John Adams. You will also learn about the hotly contested election that brought Adams to the presidency.

Link to this Internet site from http://www.myreportlinks.com

▶ ***Amistad* Trials 1839–1840**    *EDITOR'S CHOICE
This site provides extensive information about the *Amistad* trials. You can read newspaper accounts and biographies of the trial participants and view maps of the voyage.

Link to this Internet site from http://www.myreportlinks.com

▶ **The American Presidency: John Quincy Adams**    *EDITOR'S CHOICE
Grolier's American Presidency series profiles Adams. Learn how Adams felt about his presidency and his career in Congress thereafter.

Link to this Internet site from http://www.myreportlinks.com

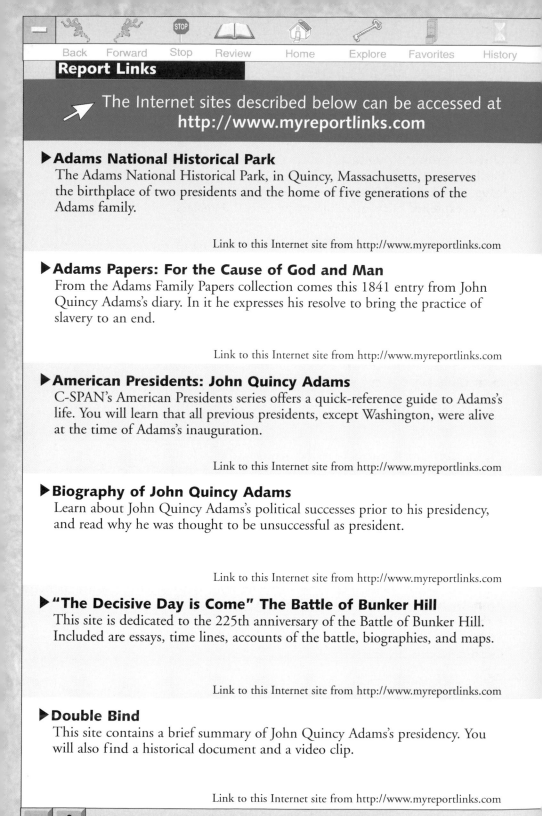

## Report Links

The Internet sites described below can be accessed at
**http://www.myreportlinks.com**

▶**Adams National Historical Park**
The Adams National Historical Park, in Quincy, Massachusetts, preserves the birthplace of two presidents and the home of five generations of the Adams family.

Link to this Internet site from http://www.myreportlinks.com

▶**Adams Papers: For the Cause of God and Man**
From the Adams Family Papers collection comes this 1841 entry from John Quincy Adams's diary. In it he expresses his resolve to bring the practice of slavery to an end.

Link to this Internet site from http://www.myreportlinks.com

▶**American Presidents: John Quincy Adams**
C-SPAN's American Presidents series offers a quick-reference guide to Adams's life. You will learn that all previous presidents, except Washington, were alive at the time of Adams's inauguration.

Link to this Internet site from http://www.myreportlinks.com

▶**Biography of John Quincy Adams**
Learn about John Quincy Adams's political successes prior to his presidency, and read why he was thought to be unsuccessful as president.

Link to this Internet site from http://www.myreportlinks.com

▶**"The Decisive Day is Come" The Battle of Bunker Hill**
This site is dedicated to the 225th anniversary of the Battle of Bunker Hill. Included are essays, time lines, accounts of the battle, biographies, and maps.

Link to this Internet site from http://www.myreportlinks.com

▶**Double Bind**
This site contains a brief summary of John Quincy Adams's presidency. You will also find a historical document and a video clip.

Link to this Internet site from http://www.myreportlinks.com

## Report Links

The Internet sites described below can be accessed at
## http://www.myreportlinks.com

▶ **"I Do Solemnly Swear..."**
The Library of Congress Web site contains John Quincy Adams's Inaugural Address, his writings in the Senate Executive Journal, and his ideas as expressed in congressional documents and debates.

Link to this Internet site from http://www.myreportlinks.com

▶ **Infoplease.com: John Quincy Adams**
John Quincy Adams based his decisions on what he thought was right, which was not always consistent with the Federalist point of view. Consequently, Adams's support of the Louisiana Purchase and the Embargo Act cost him his seat in the Senate.

Link to this Internet site from http://www.myreportlinks.com

▶ **John Quincy Adams**
This interesting profile of John Quincy Adams is an excerpt from a book titled *Arguing About Slavery*, by William Lee Miller.

Link to this Internet site from http://www.myreportlinks.com

▶ **John Quincy Adams (1767–1848)**
Two John Quincy Adams portraits hang in Washington's National Portrait Gallery. One is an oil painting by George Caleb Bingham, and the other is a daguerreotype taken in New York City.

Link to this Internet site from http://www.myreportlinks.com

▶ **John Quincy Adams: An Anti-Slavery President?**
In this excerpt from *African Americans & the Presidency*, author Christopher B. Booker suggests that Adams's antislavery principles did little to affect his policy.

Link to this Internet site from http://www.myreportlinks.com

▶ **John Quincy Adams, the Gag Rule, and the Declaration of Independence**
This essay explores the arguments of Adams and others who tried to persuade the House of Representatives that slavery was inconsistent with the ideals expressed in the Declaration of Independence.

Link to this Internet site from http://www.myreportlinks.com

## Report Links

➤ The Internet sites described below can be accessed at
**http://www.myreportlinks.com**

▶**John Quincy Adams: Inaugural Address**
From Bartleby.com's vast electronic library comes the text of John Quincy Adams's Inaugural Address. In his speech, Adams praised the record of James Monroe and pledged to continue his policies.

Link to this Internet site from http://www.myreportlinks.com

▶**John Quincy Adams, Sixth President**
This site contains a brief overview of John Quincy Adams's life and presidency as well as Adams's Inaugural Address and election results.

Link to this Internet site from http://www.myreportlinks.com

▶**Letters on the Masonic Institution**
Perhaps prompted by the alleged abduction and murder of William Morgan in 1826, John Quincy Adams a few years later voiced his strong objections to Freemasonry. This site holds the text of Adams's essay first published in 1847.

Link to this Internet site from http://www.myreportlinks.com

▶**The John Quincy Adams State Drawing Room**
A portrait of John Quincy Adams as minister to Great Britain dominates the State Department dining room named in his honor. This State Department site offers a virtual tour of the room and provides a history of the room's furnishings.

Link to this Internet site from http://www.myreportlinks.com

▶**The Monroe Doctrine Declared, 1823**
The Monroe Doctrine was largely the work of John Quincy Adams, who served as Monroe's secretary of state. This brief profile offers some fascinating background about this legendary policy.

Link to this Internet site from http://www.myreportlinks.com

▶**National Archives and Records Administration: The *Amistad* Case**
This site provides background information on the *Amistad* case. In particular, you will learn how fifty-three Africans seized the *Amistad*.

Link to this Internet site from http://www.myreportlinks.com

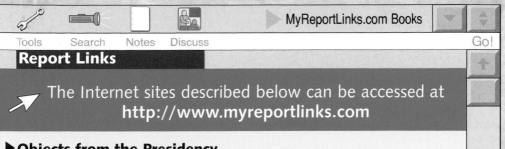
The Internet sites described below can be accessed at
http://www.myreportlinks.com

▶**Objects from the Presidency**
By navigating through this site you will find objects related to all the
United States presidents, including John Quincy Adams. You can also
read a brief description of Adams, the era he lived in, and learn about
the office of the presidency.

Link to this Internet site from http://www.myreportlinks.com

▶**The Office of the Clerk: John Quincy Adams**
Learn about the election of 1824 and the secret ballots that placed
Adams into the presidency.

Link to this Internet site from http://www.myreportlinks.com

▶**President John Quincy Adams**
This biography, written before George W. Bush's election, cites Adams
as the only son of a president to be elected to the office. You will also
learn that Adams's Tariff of 1828 probably sabotaged his chances for
reelection.

Link to this Internet site from http://www.myreportlinks.com

▶**U.S. Capitol Historical Society: John Quincy Adams's
Congressional Career**
Learn how John Quincy Adams became involved in the slavery debate
and how he brought this debate to the attention of the House.

Link to this Internet site from http://www.myreportlinks.com

▶**Visiting John Quincy Adams's Grave**
This site contains a biography of John Quincy Adams and a picture of
his gravesite, in Quincy, Massachusetts.

Link to this Internet site from http://www.myreportlinks.com

▶**The White House: Louisa Catherine Johnson Adams**
Born in London to an American father and English mother, Louisa
Catherine Johnson Adams was the only first lady born outside the
United States. The official White House site tells of her marriage to
John Quincy Adams in 1794.

Link to this Internet site from http://www.myreportlinks.com

## Highlights

**1767**—*July 11:* Born in Braintree (now Quincy), Massachusetts.

**1787**—Graduates from Harvard.

**1794**—Appointed minister to the Netherlands by President Washington.

**1797**—*July 26:* Marries Louisa Catherine Johnson.

Appointed minister to Prussia by his father, President John Adams.

**1802**—Elected to Massachusetts State Senate.

**1803**—Elected U.S. senator from Massachusetts.

**1809**—Appointed minister to Russia by President Madison.

**1814**—*December 24:* Negotiates Treaty of Ghent, ending War of 1812.

**1815**—Appointed minister to Britain.

**1817**—Appointed secretary of state by President Monroe.

**1824**—Elected sixth president of the United States.

**1828**—Defeated in reelection attempt by Andrew Jackson.

**1830**—Elected to U.S. House of Representatives.

**1841**—Successfully argues for the freedom of the slaves that had taken control of the ship *Amistad.*

**1848**—*Feb. 23:* Dies in the U.S. Capitol building.

# "Old Man Eloquent"

**S**eventy-four-year-old John Quincy Adams was worried. The aging congressman, and former United States president, was about to argue a case before the U.S. Supreme Court. Adams had not tried a case in more than thirty years. Yet, in 1839, he became involved in the *Amistad* case.

## ▶ An Interesting Dilemma

Earlier that year, a group of Africans was kidnapped and forced aboard the Spanish slave ship *Amistad*. While on board, they revolted and gained control of the ship, which was sailing off the coast of Cuba. When they directed the ship's Spanish navigator to sail back to Africa, he instead steered the ship north, to the waters off Long Island, New York. The Africans were captured there and then imprisoned in Connecticut. Soon they found themselves caught in a web of national and international politics.

Slavery was still legal in the United States in 1839. President Martin Van Buren had a difficult decision to make. He feared that if he freed the prisoners and sent them back to Africa, he would anger slaveholders. But if he sent the Africans back to Cuba, where they had been brought to be sold into slavery, he would anger the abolitionists (people opposed to slavery). So he decided to let the courts settle the matter. When the lawyers representing the African prisoners approached John Quincy Adams, he could not refuse to help.

▲ *In the center of this illustration, the slave ship* Amistad *is pictured with tattered sails. In the foreground, some of the Africans that had been held on the ship are seen bargaining for water and supplies from people on shore, in Long Island, New York.*

For the past few years, Adams had been waging a brave, but lonely, battle in Congress against the "gag rule," which kept antislavery petitions from being debated in the House. Time and again, Adams had read antislavery petitions in Congress, over the protests of southern congressmen, knowing full well that the gag rule prevented any discussion of such petitions. Adams's strenuous efforts and impassioned readings had won him the nickname "Old Man Eloquent."

## ▶ Against the Slave Trade

When the *Amistad* case came to him, however, Adams was afraid he would not have enough strength to make a convincing presentation of his arguments in court. He wrote in his diary:

> What can I, upon the verge of my seventy-fourth birthday, with a shaking hand, a darkening eye, a drowsy brain, and with my faculties dropping from me one by one, as the teeth are dropping from my head—what can I do for the cause of God and man, for the progress of human emancipation, for the suppression of the African slave-trade? Yet my conscience presses me on; let me but die upon the breach.[1]

When the case opened on February 22, 1841, Henry D. Gilpin argued on behalf of the U.S. government. He said that the Africans were slaves and therefore should be

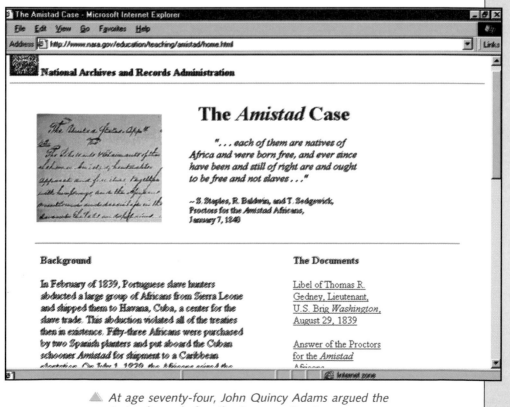

At age seventy-four, John Quincy Adams argued the Amistad *case* before the Supreme Court.

returned to Spain in accordance with a treaty between the two countries. Roger S. Baldwin argued for the defense that the Spaniards had failed to prove they owned the Africans. On the morning of February 24, Adams argued the moral issues of the case before the Court for four and a half hours.

On March 9, the Supreme Court justices ruled that the *Amistad* captives were to be set free immediately. The Court concluded that the Africans had been justified in taking over the *Amistad* because they had the same rights as any other people to resist oppression. Adams was delighted at the outcome. Soon "Old Man Eloquent" was back in Congress, battling the gag rule again. Three years later, in 1844, the restrictive rule was finally repealed by the House.

# Early Years, 1767–1790

John Quincy Adams was born on July 11, 1767, at his family's home in Braintree (later renamed Quincy), Massachusetts. He was the second of five children born to John Adams (America's second president) and Abigail Smith Adams. During the first few years of John Quincy's life, his father was active in politics and was often away from home.

## ▶ Revolutionary Era

At that time, many people in Massachusetts and in the other colonies were growing angry at their British rulers. The colonists deeply resented the taxes that the British Parliament had imposed on them. John Adams was one of the leading political thinkers who believed that the time had come to declare independence from Britain.

Both parents wanted their son to receive a good education, so Abigail Adams tutored her preschooler. By the age of six, John Quincy was already taking his education seriously. In fact, he criticized himself for not studying enough. In a letter to his young cousin Betsy Church, he wrote that he spent too much of his time in play, leaving "a great deal of room for me to grow better."[1]

In 1775, when it had reached time to send John Quincy to school, John and Abigail decided instead to continue to teach him at home. Adams had his two law clerks tutor young John Quincy in the Adamses' home. With thousands of British troops stationed in nearby Boston and the threat of war approaching, they feared it might not be safe in the surrounding towns.

The Adamses' decision to teach John Quincy at home proved to be a wise one. On April 19, 1775, British troops in Lexington, Massachusetts, fired what came to be known as the "shot heard round the world," at a force of minute-men. That was the name given to colonial patriots in the area who had been training to fight the British. The Revolutionary War had begun.

On June 17, 1775, the second battle of the war was fought. That day, John Quincy heard what sounded like thunder rumbling across the skies of Boston, to the north.

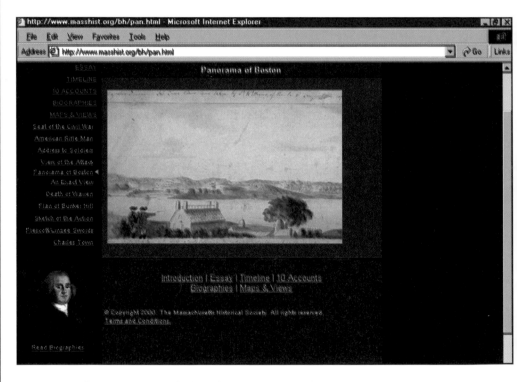

ESSAY
TIMELINE
10 ACCOUNTS
BIOGRAPHIES
MAPS & VIEWS
Seat of the Civil War
American Rifle Man
Address to Soldiers
View of the Attack
Panorama of Boston ◄
An Exact View
Death of Warren
Plan of Bunker Hill
Sketch of the Action
Prescott/Linzee Swords
Charles Town

Panorama of Boston

Introduction | Essay | Timeline | 10 Accounts
Biographies | Maps & Views

© Copyright 2003 The Massachusetts Historical Society. All rights reserved.
Terms and Conditions.

Read Biographies

▲ *A panorama of colonial Boston is pictured. On June 17, 1775, young John Quincy Adams and his mother, Abigail, climbed to the top of Penn's Hill. The thunder they thought they had heard earlier was really the roar of cannons being fired in the Battle of Bunker Hill, which was taking place not far away. It was a day that John Quincy Adams would never forget.*

Abigail and her son climbed to the top of nearby Penn's Hill, where they could see all of the countryside between Braintree and Boston. John Quincy would remember for the rest of his life what he saw that day. Smoke rose from Bunker Hill near Boston. The "thunder" they heard was really the roar of cannons. The Adamses later learned that although the British had outnumbered the colonists two to one and had won the battle, they had lost about one thousand men, twice as many as the colonists.

While the Battle of Bunker Hill was raging, John Adams was participating in the Second Continental Congress in Philadelphia. Just over a year later, on July 4, 1776, Adams and the other delegates of the Continental Congress adopted the Declaration of Independence. Now there was no turning back. The Continental Army would face an enemy that was overwhelmingly stronger, but the American colonies were now determined to win their freedom whatever the cost.

## Overseas Journey

By November 1777, the Americans needed help. The Continental Congress voted to send John Adams to France where he would join Benjamin Franklin and Arthur Lee in seeking French support for the war. Adams took ten-year-old John Quincy with him to Europe. Father and son boarded the frigate *Boston*, a small warship, on February 13, 1778.

The Atlantic crossing was both difficult and dangerous, but it was the most exciting adventure of young John Quincy's life. They were chased by a British warship, struck by lightning, caught in a hurricane, and engaged in battle with another British warship. Adams was pleased that John Quincy never complained and proud that the boy showed such courage. Finally, on April 1, the *Boston* arrived in Bordeaux, France. The six-week adventure at sea had ended safely for the Adamses.

John Quincy spent his next seven years in Europe, except for a brief trip home with his father in 1779. When the Adamses arrived in Paris, John Adams enrolled his son at the Passy Academy, just outside the city. The young American now began his first formal education. He learned French very quickly and impressed his father with his progress.

## ▶ First Trip to Russia

In 1780, John Adams transferred his son to the University of Leiden in the Netherlands. The following year, at the age of fourteen, John Quincy obtained his father's consent to accompany Francis Dana, an American diplomat, on a mission to Russia. Dana needed a private secretary and someone who could also serve as his interpreter. John Quincy spoke fluent French, which was the language used for diplomacy at the Russian court.

On July 7, 1781, John Quincy and Dana began their two-thousand-mile overland journey to St. Petersburg, the Russian capital at the time. John Quincy believed the Russian capital to be the most beautiful city he had ever seen. After John Quincy had spent more than a year in St. Petersburg, his father decided that it was time for him to leave Russia. So on October 30, 1782, John Quincy set off by himself on a journey back to the Netherlands. He traveled over the snow-covered countryside of Finland, Sweden, Denmark, and Prussia (Germany) and journeyed part of the way by boat.

Finally, on April 21, John Quincy, a young man not quite sixteen years old, arrived in The Hague, the Netherlands. John Adams, taking leave from peace talks with the British in Paris, joined his son at The Hague on July 22. Offered the choice of returning to the University of Leiden or studying privately with his father, John Quincy chose to stay with his father. The next year, John Quincy served as an assistant secretary to the American representatives in Paris who were still negotiating a peace treaty with Britain. On September 3, 1783, the American and British negotiators signed the Treaty of Paris, formally ending the Revolutionary War.

John Quincy's father stayed in Paris to negotiate trade treaties and then returned to the Netherlands to arrange for a loan for the American government. John Quincy

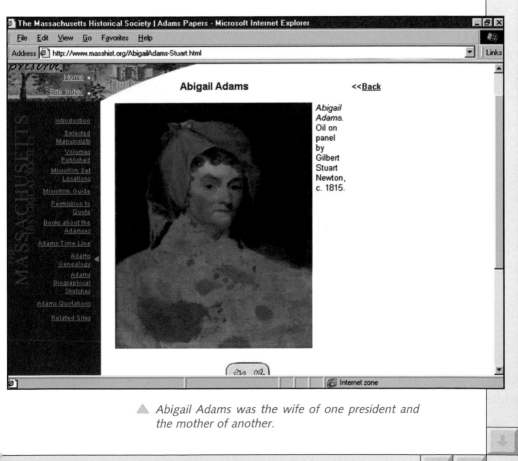

▲ Abigail Adams was the wife of one president and the mother of another.

served as his father's private secretary while also continuing his studies. In 1784, he greeted his mother, Abigail, and his sister Nabby when they arrived in London.

## A Return Home

In 1785, John Quincy returned to America to enter Harvard College in Cambridge, Massachusetts, as a junior. Although he had enjoyed his European education, he now felt drawn to the home he had not seen since the age of twelve. In a burst of patriotism, he wrote, "No person who has not experienced it can conceive how much pleasure there is in returning to our country after an absence of seven years, especially when it was left at the time of life that I did."[2]

John Quincy graduated from Harvard in July 1787, second in a class of fifty-one graduates. For the next three years, he studied law under Theophilus Parsons, in Newburyport, Massachusetts. In July 1790, John Quincy Adams was admitted to the Massachusetts bar—the state's association of lawyers and other legal professionals.

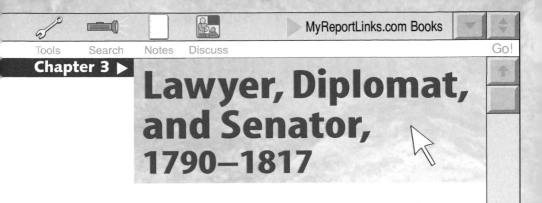
## Chapter 3 ▶

# Lawyer, Diplomat, and Senator, 1790–1817

John Quincy Adams seemed to be following in his father's footsteps, which was what John Adams had always expected of his son. Both father and son had graduated from Harvard and become lawyers. John Adams had gone on to become a diplomat, representing the United States abroad. In 1789, when George Washington became the first president of the United States, John Adams returned to America to become the new nation's first vice president. He would become America's second president, in 1797.

## ▶ A Different Path?

John Quincy Adams, however, became bored with the legal profession and had no interest in becoming a politician. In fact, he was more interested in becoming a poet. Still, he was an obedient son and tried to follow the career path his parents had laid out for him.

In 1789, while still living in Newburyport, John Quincy Adams fell in love with a young woman named Mary Frazier, but since he was not in a position to support a family, he decided to end their relationship. Many years later, John Quincy Adams wrote in a diary entry dated November 18, 1838, "Dearly! how dearly did the sacrifice of her cost me, voluntary as it was. . . . four years of exquisite wretchedness followed . . . nor was the wound in my bosom healed till the Atlantic Ocean flowed between us."[1]

In 1791, the unhappy young lawyer put his failed romance out of his mind by writing a series of political essays, called "Letters of Publicola." These were published as letters in Boston's *Columbian Centinel*. Each letter was signed "Publicola," Latin for "friend of the people." In one essay, Adams argued forcefully against the ideas of Thomas Paine in Paine's pamphlet called *The Rights of Man*. Paine, defending the French Revolution, argued that the British government could learn from the French example. John Quincy Adams's essays became popular and were even reprinted in several countries. By 1794, John Quincy Adams had decided against continuing a career in law. He grew more determined than ever to avoid a political career and live his life as he wanted, not as his parents wanted.

*The son of John Adams wanted to avoid a life in politics. But a young John Quincy Adams, pictured here, soon followed in his father's footsteps by being appointed a foreign minister.*

## Minister to the Netherlands

Just as John Quincy Adams was about to follow a different career path, his father told him that George Washington intended to appoint John Quincy the U.S. minister to the Netherlands. John Quincy Adams was not pleased by the appointment. He complained, "I wish I could have been consulted before it was irrevocably made . . . I rather wish it had not been made at all."[2] Still, it was an offer that he accepted.

In September 1794, John Quincy Adams sailed out of Boston Harbor aboard the *Alfred*. Accompanying him was his younger brother Thomas, who served as his secretary. The Adams brothers reached England on October 15, after almost a month of seasickness during the stormy Atlantic crossing. John Quincy Adams's first diplomatic task was to deliver important papers to John Jay in London. At the time, Jay, the chief justice of the United States, was negotiating a treaty with Britain.

When the Adams brothers arrived in The Hague, the Netherlands, they found a country at war. French troops occupied the city. John Quincy Adams spent his time there sizing up the situation and sending reports back to America. When he returned to London, he spent some time with John Jay and Thomas Pinckney, the U.S. minister to Britain. They discussed aspects of the treaty that Jay was negotiating, which would become known as the Jay Treaty.

While in London, John Quincy Adams met Louisa Catherine Johnson, the daughter of Joshua Johnson, a Maryland businessman, and Katherine Nuth Johnson, an Englishwoman. Before returning to the Netherlands in 1796, he declared his love for Louisa, and the two became engaged. The following year, George Washington

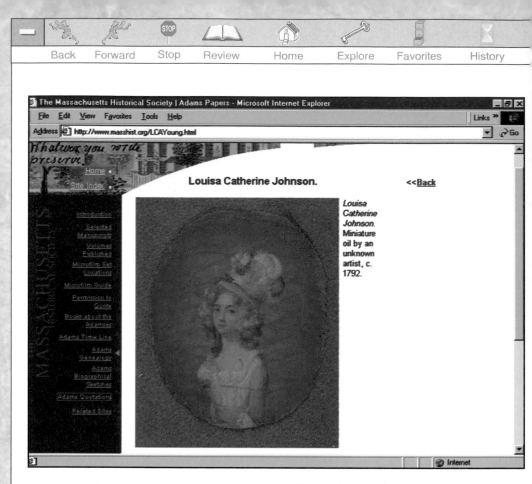

In the browser window:

**Louisa Catherine Johnson.**     <<Back

*Louisa Catherine Johnson. Miniature oil by an unknown artist, c. 1792.*

Browser chrome text:

Back | Forward | Stop | Review | Home | Explore | Favorites | History

The Massachusetts Historical Society | Adams Papers - Microsoft Internet Explorer

File  Edit  View  Favorites  Tools  Help          Links »

Address http://www.masshist.org/LCAYoung.html          Go

*Whatever you write preserve*

Home
Site Index

Introduction
Selected Manuscripts
Volumes Published
Microfilm Set Locations
Microfilm Guide
Permission to Quote
Books about the Adamses
Adams Time Line
Adams Genealogy
Adams Biographical Sketches
Adams Quotations
Related Sites

Internet

▲ *John Quincy Adams and Louisa Catherine Johnson were married on July 26, 1797, in the parish church of All Hallows Barking, in London, England.*

appointed John Quincy Adams minister to Portugal. Before John Quincy Adams could begin his new assignment, however, his father, John Adams, became president. Adams reassigned his son as minister to Prussia.

On July 26, 1797, before he left for Berlin, John Quincy Adams and Louisa Catherine Johnson were married. In Berlin, Adams succeeded in negotiating a treaty between Prussian king Frederick William III's government and the United States.

In 1801, Thomas Jefferson was elected the next U.S. president, and John Adams retired to Quincy,

Massachusetts. In the spring of 1801, John Quincy Adams and his wife also returned to Massachusetts, where Adams would begin a new type of public service. The following year he was elected to the Massachusetts State Senate to represent Suffolk County.

## U.S. Senator

Two years later, in 1803, John Quincy Adams was elected to the U.S. Senate by the Federalist-controlled Massachusetts legislature. In the Senate, he demonstrated that he was an independent thinker who did what he believed was right, not what the Federalist leaders demanded. Adams was the only Federalist to support President Jefferson's Republican policies and decisions.

In 1807, the New England Federalists in the Senate were furious when John Quincy Adams helped pass Jefferson's Embargo Act. He had joined Jefferson in responding to British interference with American shipping. The Embargo Act made it illegal for American ships to sail to foreign ports. It also severely cut down on the number of boats that could unload their goods in American ports.

John Quincy Adams said that in defense of the rights of American sailors, he "was ready, if necessary, to sacrifice every thing I have in life, and even life itself."[3] Adams proved, as he would on many other occasions, that he was more concerned with justice than politics. Unfortunately, the shipping industry in the northeastern United States was crippled by the Embargo Act, and many people lost their jobs. In June 1808, after losing Federalist support in Massachusetts, John Quincy Adams resigned his Senate seat.

As the first U.S. minister to Russia, John Quincy Adams reported on Napoléon's successful campaigns in that country as well as on his retreat from Moscow. In this painting, the self-proclaimed emperor of France is pictured on a battlefield in France.

## Minister to Russia

The following year, President James Madison appointed Adams to be the first U.S. minister to Russia. On August 5, 1809, accompanied by his wife Louisa, his two-year-old son Charles Francis, three secretaries, and two servants, he set sail on the *Horace*, bound for St. Petersburg, which they reached on October 22. His two older sons remained behind with relatives. It would be eight years before John Quincy Adams again set foot on American soil.

He recalled that on his previous stay in St. Petersburg, nearly thirty years before, he and Francis Dana had been, for the most part, ignored by the Russian court. This time things were very different. The thirty-two-year-old czar

Alexander I, ten years younger than John Quincy Adams, took an interest in the American diplomat. The friendship that developed between Czar Alexander and Adams no doubt played a role in the Russian agreement to open the Baltic Sea to American shipping.

In 1811, President Madison recommended John Quincy Adams to fill a seat that had become vacant on the U.S. Supreme Court. But Adams turned down the honor. He used his wife's pregnancy as an excuse, saying her condition made it impossible for them to travel.

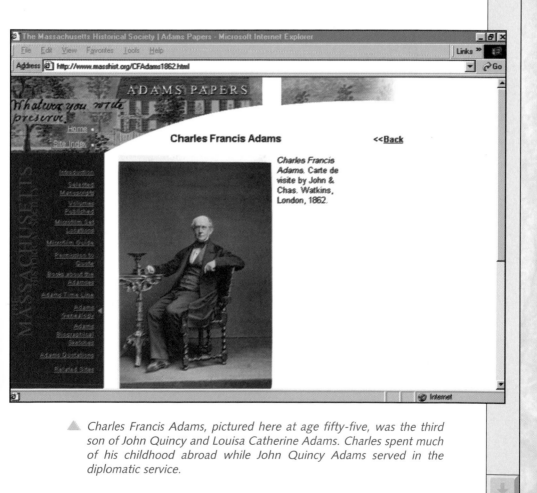

▲ *Charles Francis Adams, pictured here at age fifty-five, was the third son of John Quincy and Louisa Catherine Adams. Charles spent much of his childhood abroad while John Quincy Adams served in the diplomatic service.*

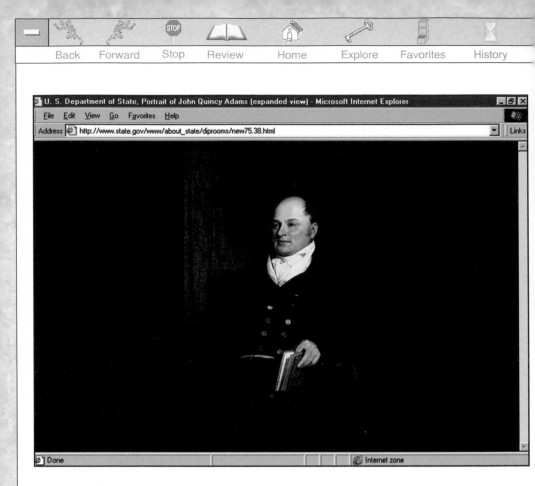

U. S. Department of State, Portrait of John Quincy Adams (expanded view) - Microsoft Internet Explorer

File    Edit    View    Go    Favorites    Help

Address  http://www.state.gov/www/about_state/diprooms/new75.38.html    ▼  Links

Done                                    Internet zone

▲ *This portrait of John Quincy Adams was painted in 1816
while Adams served as the minister to Great Britain.*

Later that year, the Adamses were thrilled when Louisa
gave birth to a girl, whom they named Louisa Catherine.

The next year, 1812, proved to be one of tragedy for
the Adamses. Their baby daughter became ill and died. On
the international level, Russia became engulfed in war in
April. Russia's former ally Napoléon Bonaparte, ruler of
France, turned against the Russians and launched a
massive invasion. And in June, the U.S. Congress declared
war against Britain, in what would become known as the
War of 1812. Throughout this difficult period, John
Quincy Adams helped to maintain good relations between

the United States and Russia. That was not an easy task because Russia's new enemy, France, was also the enemy of Britain, and Britain was once again the enemy of the United States.

John Quincy Adams sent back firsthand accounts of Russia's readiness for war. He also made frequent reports on Napoléon's initial successes and then announced Napoléon's retreat from Moscow. By 1814, the United States and Britain had reached a stalemate and were ready to end their war. President Madison appointed Adams to head a five-man delegation to negotiate a peace treaty with

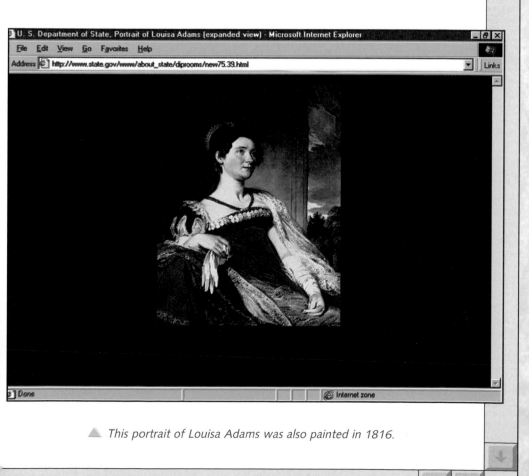

U. S. Department of State, Portrait of Louisa Adams (expanded view) - Microsoft Internet Explorer

File  Edit  View  Go  Favorites  Help

Address  http://www.state.gov/www/about_state/diprooms/new75.39.html          Links

Done                                                      Internet zone

▲ *This portrait of Louisa Adams was also painted in 1816.*

Britain. In June 1814, Adams arrived in Ghent, Belgium, the site of the negotiations.

## ▶ Treaty of Ghent

On December 24, 1814, the United States and Britain signed the Treaty of Ghent. Although the treaty officially ended the War of 1812, news of the signing unfortunately did not reach the United States until February 11, 1815. So the final battle of the War of 1812, the Battle of New Orleans, was fought on January 8, 1815, two weeks after the signing of the treaty.

Adams next went to Paris, where he was joined by his wife and son. In May 1815, Adams was named minister to Great Britain. Once the Adamses were situated in London, their two oldest sons, George and John, sailed from America to unite the family.

In 1816, James Monroe was elected the fifth American president. In 1817, he appointed John Quincy Adams as his secretary of state. Monroe believed that no American had better knowledge of, or more experience in, foreign affairs than John Quincy Adams. In June 1817, the Adamses again crossed the Atlantic, this time bound for New York.

**Chapter 4** ▶

# Secretary of State, 1817–1825

The Adamses took up residence in Washington, D.C., in September 1817. John Quincy Adams immediately went to work in the administration of President James Monroe. With the end of the War of 1812, the American economy strengthened and the nation experienced a time of relative prosperity. It was a period known as the "Era of Good Feeling."

Nevertheless, serious problems were about to begin. In 1817 and 1818, reports reached Washington about murderous attacks upon settlers in southern Georgia by bands of Seminole Indians. After each attack, the Seminole would slip back across the border into Spanish Florida. There, on foreign soil, they were safe from pursuit.

## ▶ Role as Secretary of State

In the spring of 1818, General Andrew Jackson, the hero of the Battle of New Orleans, led an army into Spanish Florida. Because the Spanish had done nothing to end the Seminole attacks, President Monroe authorized Jackson to use military force to defend the white settlers living near the border of Spanish Florida. Jackson went farther, however, invading the Spanish territory. Jackson's troops attacked Seminole villages and showed no mercy. What became known as the First Seminole War ended in victory for the American troops.

The Spanish ambassador, Don Luís de Onís y Gonzales, demanded that Jackson be punished for his invasion of Spanish territory. All of Monroe's advisors with the exception of Adams urged the president to do so. Adams, though angry with Jackson, supported Jackson's actions. He argued that Spain was to blame for the situation in Florida. Adams believed that the best course for the United States was to negotiate the purchase of Florida from Spain. President Monroe agreed, and by the following year, Adams had concluded negotiations with Ambassador Onís. On February 22, 1819, Adams and Onís signed an agreement, which became known as the Adams-Onís Treaty. According to the terms of the treaty, Florida was ceded to the United States at a total cost of $5 million—not in money paid to Spain but in money paid to American citizens who had legal claims against Spain.

Later that year, a new problem emerged. Missouri, a territory west of the Mississippi, with a growing population of settlers, had applied for statehood in 1817. In 1819, Congress was set to authorize Missouri's statehood when Representative James Tallmadge of New York tried to insert an antislavery amendment into the authorization. Up to this point, the Union was equally divided between eleven "slave" states where slavery was legal and eleven "free" states where it was not. Naturally, Northerners wanted Missouri to be admitted to the Union as a free state, and Southerners wanted it to be a slave state. Should slavery be confined to the South, or should it be allowed to spread to the West? Heated debate over the issue continued in Congress through part of the following year. Some Southerners spoke openly about leaving the Union.

A proposal for a compromise came from Senator Jesse Thomas of Illinois. In March of 1820 he proposed that Maine be admitted as a free state and Missouri as a slave state to maintain the balance. As part of the "Missouri Compromise," any western territory north of Missouri's southern border would be considered "free" soil. Maine became a free state in 1820, and Missouri a slave state in 1821.

Although Adams detested slavery, considering it an "outrage upon the goodness of God,"[1] he supported the Missouri Compromise. He believed that it was the only way to keep the Union together.

Adams continued as secretary of state during Monroe's second administration. As prosperity continued and the

Monroe Doctrine - Microsoft Internet Explorer

File    Edit    View    Go    Favorites    Help

Address http://campus.northpark.edu/history/Classes/Sources/Monroe.html    Links

## *The Monroe Doctrine*

*James Monroe (1758-1831) delivered this speech to a joint session of Congress in which he outlined his foreign policy objectives. This speech can be seen as the part of the United States's response to the Napoleonic Wars and to the revolution in Latin America.*

Washington, *December 2, 1823.*

*Fellow-Citizens of the Senate and House of Representatives::*

Many important subjects will claim your attention during the present session, of which I shall endeavor to give, in aid of your deliberations, a just idea in this communication. I undertake this duty with diffidence, from the vast extent of the interests on which I have to treat and of their great importance to every portion of our Union. I enter on it with zeal from a thorough conviction that there never was a period since the establishment of our Revolution when, regarding the condition of the civilized world and its bearing on us, there was greater necessity for devotion in the public servants to their respective duties, or for virtue, patriotism, and union in our constituents.

Meeting in you a new Congress, I deem it proper to present this view of public affairs in greater detail than might otherwise be necessary. I do it, however, with peculiar satisfaction, from a knowledge that in this respect I shall comply more fully with the sound principles of our Government. The people being with us exclusively the sovereign, it is indispensable that full information be laid before them on all important subjects, to enable them to exercise that high power with complete effect. If kept in the dark, they must be incompetent to it. We are all liable to error, and those who are engaged in the management of public affairs are more subject to excitement and to be

Internet zone

As secretary of state to President James Monroe, Adams was the driving force behind the Monroe Doctrine.

nation grew stronger, Americans turned their attention to struggles for freedom that were being waged in other parts of the hemisphere. Monroe urged Congress to recognize the independence of Colombia, Chile, Peru, Mexico, and Argentina, formerly held by Spain.

## Monroe Doctrine

But there was concern that Spain would try to recapture its former colonies in South America, and that Russia, which still owned Alaska, might try to expand in the Oregon Territory. Secretary of State Adams advised President Monroe to announce that any nation interfering in the Western Hemisphere would risk war with the United States. In 1823, Adams wrote a policy statement for Monroe, which became known as the Monroe Doctrine. The Monroe Doctrine became the foundation for the United States' foreign policy for North and South America.

For a while, Adams was gratified to have helped the United States emerge as a world power, but his role as secretary of state fell short of his ambitions. He now dreamed that somehow he might be chosen as the next U.S. president. As the nation's leader, he believed he could accomplish wonderful things for America and the world.

**Chapter 5 ▶**

# America's Sixth President, 1825–1829

The campaign leading up to the presidential election of 1824 had been particularly bitter for Adams. His political enemies attacked him in the press. They made fun of his stiff personality and formal manner—even of the way he dressed. Adams was stung by the disrespectful treatment he

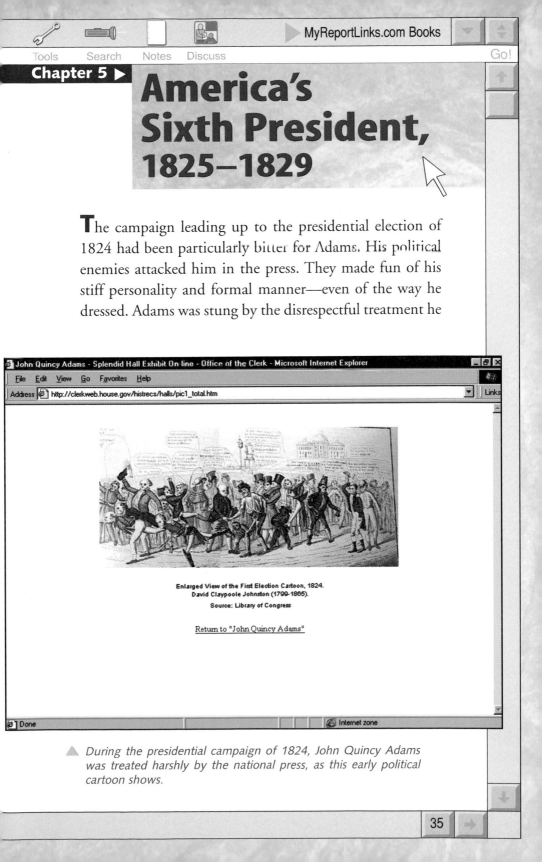

John Quincy Adams - Splendid Hall Exhibit On line - Office of the Clerk - Microsoft Internet Explorer

File   Edit   View   Go   Favorites   Help

Address  http://clerkweb.house.gov/histrecs/halls/pic1_total.htm          Links

Enlarged View of the First Election Cartoon, 1824.
David Claypoole Johnston (1799-1865).
Source: Library of Congress

Return to "John Quincy Adams"

Done                                              Internet zone

▲ During the presidential campaign of 1824, John Quincy Adams was treated harshly by the national press, as this early political cartoon shows.

received in the newspapers. He was honest about what others saw as his shortcomings, admitting, "I am a man of reserved, cold, austere, and forbidding manners."[1] Nevertheless, the attacks continued.

## ▶ A Split Decision

Adams's main opponents in the race were Andrew Jackson of Tennessee, William Crawford of Georgia, and Henry Clay of Kentucky. John C. Calhoun of South Carolina had dropped out early on and was running for vice president instead. Although Adams had strong support in New England and New York, Jackson got the largest number of popular votes and the most electoral votes. However, because none of the candidates received a majority of the electoral votes, it fell to the House of Representatives to choose the president. They chose from the three candidates with the highest number of electoral votes: Jackson with ninety-nine, Adams with eighty-four, and Crawford with forty-one.

Henry Clay, who had received only thirty-seven electoral votes, was dropped from the race. But as Speaker of the House, he had a great deal of influence in Congress. To the outrage of many members of Congress, Clay chose to support Adams. As a result, Adams was elected president, and John C. Calhoun became vice president.

At his inauguration on March 4, 1825, fifty-seven-year-old John Quincy Adams took the oath of office from Chief Justice John Marshall. In his inaugural speech, Adams was humble and grateful. He was aware that he had become president by winning neither the popular vote nor the electoral vote. He promised that he would carry out his presidential duties with the best intentions.

On April 25, the Adamses moved into the President's House (the White House). Adams entered the presidency with high hopes of making the United States a better place. During the next four years he proposed such federally funded programs as the construction of new roads and canals to improve transportation and commerce, the building of an astronomical observatory, and the establishment of a national university. To his regret, a hostile Congress, full of Jackson's supporters, opposed all of Adams's proposals, preventing him from accomplishing most of his goals.

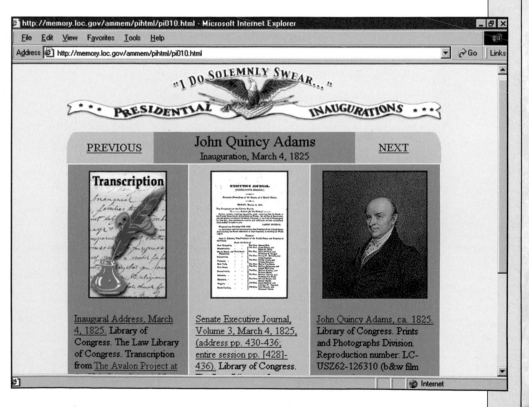

President John Quincy Adams expressed humility in his inaugural address on March 4, 1825, fully aware that he had not received the popular vote of the nation.

## ▶ Political Struggles

From practically the first day of his administration until the last, Adams's political enemies in Congress, and there were many, constantly attacked him. They accused Adams of corruption when he appointed Clay secretary of state—since Clay was the man who had put him in the presidency. Jackson's supporters were furious that Adams had somehow "stolen" the election from their man.

As the four years of his presidency wore on, John Quincy Adams felt himself a victim of partisan politics.

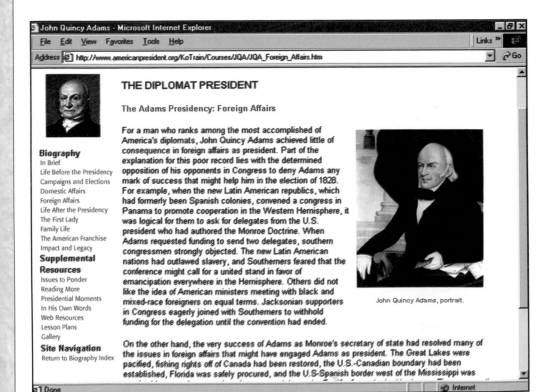

The successes that John Quincy Adams had as a diplomat were not repeated during his presidency. His opponents in Congress, mostly Jackson supporters, were determined that Adams not be reelected in1828.

 *This engraving of President John Quincy Adams shows him seated in his library, surrounded by maps and books. The studious Adams had hoped to achieve great things as president, but he was often stopped short in his efforts by a hostile Congress.*

He grew to hate Andrew Jackson. By the time Adams had become president, the old Federalist party no longer existed. All political leaders were Republicans. The Republicans, however, were now split into two factions: the National Republicans and the Democratic-Republicans (later to be known as Democrats). Adams and Clay were National Republicans—they were interested in programs that benefited the nation as a whole. Jackson and his followers were Democratic-Republicans. They supported states' rights and were interested in programs that would benefit individual states or regions.

In 1827, the issue of states' rights erupted when Georgia's Governor Troup sent surveyors into lands belonging to the Creek Indians. The action violated a federal treaty with the Creek and was the first step in Troup's plan to remove the Creek from their land. Adams threatened federal military intervention to enforce federal law. On the other hand, Democratic-Republicans in the Senate argued that since the treaty gave Georgia title to the land, the U.S. government had no right to interfere. Adams was unable to protect the rights of the Creek. They were forced to give up all claim to their land. In addition, Adams had alienated the citizens of Georgia, who would help to defeat him in the next election.

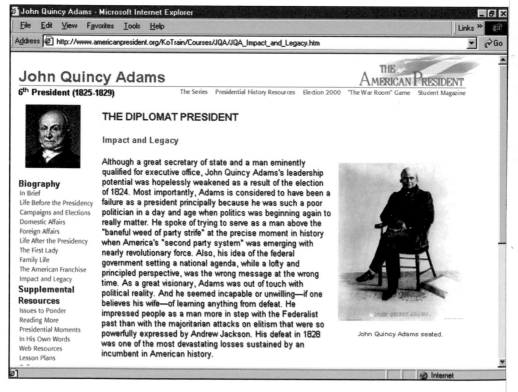

John Quincy Adams - Microsoft Internet Explorer

File    Edit    View    Favorites    Tools    Help        Links »

Address http://www.americanpresident.org/KoTrain/Courses/JQA/JQA_Impact_and_Legacy.htm        Go

# John Quincy Adams
**6th President (1825-1829)**

THE AMERICAN PRESIDENT

The Series    Presidential History Resources    Election 2000    "The War Room" Game    Student Magazine

## THE DIPLOMAT PRESIDENT

### Impact and Legacy

**Biography**
In Brief
Life Before the Presidency
Campaigns and Elections
Domestic Affairs
Foreign Affairs
Life After the Presidency
The First Lady
Family Life
The American Franchise
Impact and Legacy
**Supplemental Resources**
Issues to Ponder
Reading More
Presidential Moments
In His Own Words
Web Resources
Lesson Plans

Although a great secretary of state and a man eminently qualified for executive office, John Quincy Adams's leadership potential was hopelessly weakened as a result of the election of 1824. Most importantly, Adams is considered to have been a failure as a president principally because he was such a poor politician in a day and age when politics was beginning again to really matter. He spoke of trying to serve as a man above the "baneful weed of party strife" at the precise moment in history when America's "second party system" was emerging with nearly revolutionary force. Also, his idea of the federal government setting a national agenda, while a lofty and principled perspective, was the wrong message at the wrong time. As a great visionary, Adams was out of touch with political reality. And he seemed incapable or unwilling—if one believes his wife—of learning anything from defeat. He impressed people as a man more in step with the Federalist past than with the majoritarian attacks on elitism that were so powerfully expressed by Andrew Jackson. His defeat in 1828 was one of the most devastating losses sustained by an incumbent in American history.

John Quincy Adams seated.

Internet

▲ John Quincy Adams's accomplishments as president were overshadowed by his humiliating defeat in the election of 1828. Adams refused to attend the inauguration ceremony for the man who succeeded him as president, Andrew Jackson.

## Some Successes

Despite the unhappiness and frustration Adams experienced as president, the United States became stronger during his administration. The population grew as thousands of immigrants from Germany and Ireland poured into the country, seeking a better life. Major progress in transportation occurred when the Erie Canal—crossing New York State from Lake Erie to the Hudson River—was completed in 1825. In 1828, Adams proposed a high tariff on imported manufactured goods to protect United States industries. Despite the opposition of Jackson's supporters, the tariff became law. Adams's enemies took to calling the new law the "Tariff of Abominations."

After serving only one term, Adams was defeated by Jackson in the election of 1828. The campaign had been a bitter one. Adams received only 83 electoral votes to Jackson's 178. Adams was relieved that his four years of frustration would soon be over, but he was humiliated by the election results—so much so that he refused to attend Jackson's inauguration ceremony. By June of 1829, Adams was back in his hometown of Quincy, Massachusetts, ready to begin his years of retirement from public life.

# Chapter 6

# Later Years in Congress, 1830–1848

**A**s John Quincy Adams began his retirement in 1829, all he could recall of his past years in public service were disappointments and failures. He felt that his reputation had been ruined by the Jacksonians' attacks on his character. He quietly retired to reading and gardening, never imagining that his departure from public life would be short.

## ▶ To Congress

In August 1830, Adams received a visit from a group of local politicians who asked him to run for a seat in the U.S. House of Representatives. Though surprised by the request, he was excited by the prospect and agreed to run. That fall, he was elected to serve in Congress. In so doing, he became the only former president to return to the House of Representatives after holding the highest office. Eager to return to Washington, the sixty-three-year-old Adams said, "No election or appointment ever gave me so much pleasure. My election as president was not half so gratifying."[1]

On December 5, 1831, Adams began his work as a congressman from Massachusetts—work that would continue for seventeen years. From his first day in Congress, he angered representatives from the South by presenting petitions calling for an end to slavery. Adams continued to speak out against slavery, even after receiving death threats. Over the years Adams took part in all the major discussions in Congress, but he kept bringing up the issue of slavery. In May 1836, his opponents in the House passed a gag rule providing that antislavery petitions be "laid upon the table" without any debate allowed on them. For the next eight years, Adams fought for the freedom to discuss those petitions. In December 1844, he finally succeeded in getting enough votes to have the rule repealed.

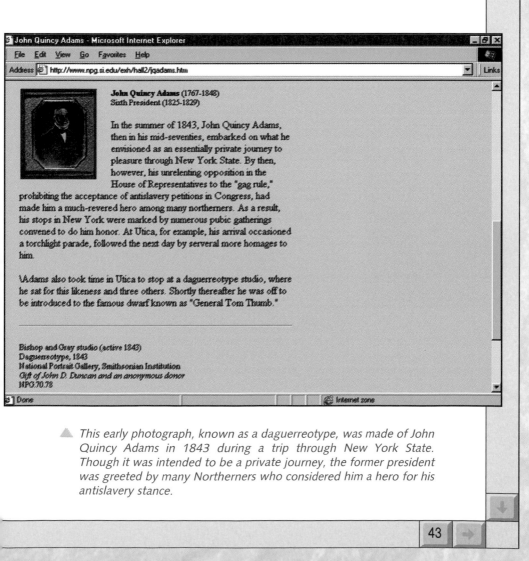

**John Quincy Adams** (1767-1848)
Sixth President (1825-1829)

In the summer of 1843, John Quincy Adams, then in his mid-seventies, embarked on what he envisioned as an essentially private journey to pleasure through New York State. By then, however, his unrelenting opposition in the House of Representatives to the "gag rule," prohibiting the acceptance of antislavery petitions in Congress, had made him a much-revered hero among many northerners. As a result, his stops in New York were marked by numerous public gatherings convened to do him honor. At Utica, for example, his arrival occasioned a torchlight parade, followed the next day by serveral more homages to him.

\Adams also took time in Utica to stop at a daguerreotype studio, where he sat for this likeness and three others. Shortly thereafter he was off to be introduced to the famous dwarf known as "General Tom Thumb."

Bishop and Gray studio (active 1843)
Daguerreotype, 1843
National Portrait Gallery, Smithsonian Institution
Gift of John D. Duncan and an anonymous donor
NPG.70.78

▲ This early photograph, known as a daguerreotype, was made of John Quincy Adams in 1843 during a trip through New York State. Though it was intended to be a private journey, the former president was greeted by many Northerners who considered him a hero for his antislavery stance.

Adams continued to fight for what he believed was right until his dying day. In 1841, he successfully argued before the Supreme Court to win freedom for the slave mutineers aboard the Spanish ship *Amistad.* He voted against the annexation of Texas and, in 1846, against the declaration of war against Mexico.

## ▶ The End of a Full Life

On November 20, 1846, Adams suffered a mild stroke. Then, on February 21, 1848, just minutes after protesting a proposal in Congress to decorate generals serving in the

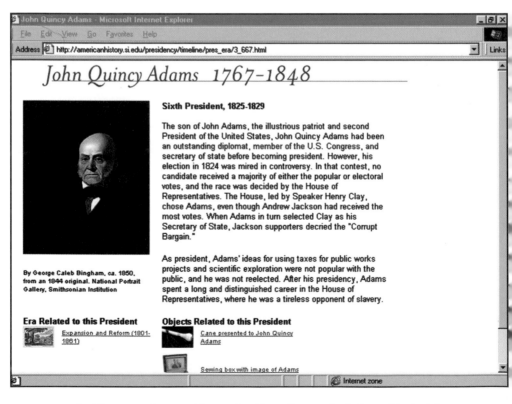

*John Quincy Adams 1767–1848*

**Sixth President, 1825-1829**

The son of John Adams, the illustrious patriot and second President of the United States, John Quincy Adams had been an outstanding diplomat, member of the U.S. Congress, and secretary of state before becoming president. However, his election in 1824 was mired in controversy. In that contest, no candidate received a majority of either the popular or electoral votes, and the race was decided by the House of Representatives. The House, led by Speaker Henry Clay, chose Adams, even though Andrew Jackson had received the most votes. When Adams in turn selected Clay as his Secretary of State, Jackson supporters decried the "Corrupt Bargain."

As president, Adams' ideas for using taxes for public works projects and scientific exploration were not popular with the public, and he was not reelected. After his presidency, Adams spent a long and distinguished career in the House of Representatives, where he was a tireless opponent of slavery.

By George Caleb Bingham, ca. 1850, from an 1844 original. National Portrait Gallery, Smithsonian Institution

**Era Related to this President** — Expansion and Reform (1801-1861)

**Objects Related to this President** — Cane presented to John Quincy Adams; Sewing box with image of Adams

▲ *The son of a president who himself was elected president, John Quincy Adams died, in 1848, in the place where he had achieved his greatest success—the U.S. Capitol.*

Mexican War, Adams suffered a massive stroke. It was determined that he was too ill to be removed from the Capitol building, so he was carried to a sofa in the Speaker's room. There, before slipping into a coma, he uttered the words "This is the end of earth. I am content."[2] Two days later, on February 23, John Quincy Adams, at the age of eighty, died in the U.S. Capitol, a place he had felt more at home in than the White House. Even his foes in Congress acknowledged the courage and integrity of the man who had served his country in so many capacities for so many years.

### Chapter 1. "Old Man Eloquent"
1. Helen Kromer, *Amistad: The Slave Uprising Aboard the Spanish Schooner* (Cleveland, Ohio: The Pilgrim Press, 1997), pp. 77–78.

### Chapter 2. Early Years, 1767–1790
1. Paul C. Nagel, *John Quincy Adams: A Public Life, a Private Life* (New York: Alfred A. Knopf, 1997), p. 11.

2. Ibid., p. 39.

### Chapter 3. Lawyer, Diplomat, and Senator, 1790–1817
1. Paul C. Nagel, *John Quincy Adams: A Public Life, a Private Life* (New York: Alfred A. Knopf, 1997), p. 69.

2. Ibid., p. 81.

3. Ibid., p. 177.

### Chapter 4. Secretary of State, 1817–1825
1. Paul C. Nagel, *John Quincy Adams: A Public Life, a Private Life* (New York: Alfred A. Knopf, 1997), p. 266.

### Chapter 5. America's Sixth President, 1825–1829
1. Samuel Flagg Bemis, *John Quincy Adams and the Foundations of American Foreign Policy* (New York: Knopf, 1949), p. 253, as quoted in *The Complete Book of U.S. Presidents* by William A. DeGregorio (New York: Wings Books, 1997), p. 89.

### Chapter 6. Later Years in Congress, 1830–1848
1. Philip B. Kunhardt, Jr., Philip B. Kunhardt III, and Peter W. Kunhardt, *The American President* (New York: Riverhead Books, 1999), p. 171.

2. Marie B. Hecht, *John Quincy Adams: A Personal History of an Independent Man* (New York: Macmillan, 1972), p. 11, as quoted in *The Complete Book of U.S. Presidents* by William A. DeGregorio (New York: Wings Books, 1997), p. 100.

## Further Reading

Freedman, Suzanne. *United States v. Amistad: Rebellion on a Slave Ship.* Berkeley Heights, N.J.: Enslow Publishers, Inc., 2000.

Greenblatt, Miriam. *John Quincy Adams: Sixth President of the United States.* Ada, Okla.: Garrett Educational Corporation, 1990.

Hecht, Marie B. *John Quincy Adams: A Personal History of an Independent Man.* New York: The Macmillan Company, 1972.

Joseph, Paul. *John Quincy Adams.* Minneapolis: ABDO Publishing Company, 1999.

Kent, Zachary. *John Quincy Adams: Sixth President of the United States.* Chicago: Children's Press, 1987.

Myers, Walter Dean. *Amistad: A Long Road to Freedom.* New York: Dutton Children's Books, 1998.

Nagel, Paul C. *John Quincy Adams: A Public Life, a Private Life.* New York: Alfred A. Knopf, 1997.

Shepherd, Jack. *The Adams Chronicles: Four Generations of Greatness.* Boston: Little, Brown and Company, 1975.

Walker, Jane C. *John Quincy Adams.* Berkeley Heights, N.J.: Enslow Publishers, Inc., 2000.

# Index